MEDITATION DEMYSTIFIED

A Reference Workbook for Everyone

Dancing Bear, Ph.D.

www.dancingbearway.com

Balboa Press books may be ordered through booksellers or by contacting:

Balboa Press
A Division of Hay House
1663 Liberty Drive
Bloomington, IN 47403
www.balboapress.com
1 (877) 407-4847

ISBN: 978-1-9822-3784-4 (sc)
ISBN: 978-1-9822-3785-1 (e)

Library of Congress Control Number: 2019917584

Print information available on the last page.

Balboa Press rev. date: 10/30/2019

BALBOA.PRESS
A DIVISION OF HAY HOUSE

Dedication:

2nd Edition "This edition is dedicated to Archangel Metatron

1st Edition "This book is dedicated to Green Tara."

When all is said and done it is the difference we make, that is our legacy.

– Dancing Bear

Table of Contents

Table of Figures

Preface to 2ⁿᵈ Edition

This book is based on the class material developed for the meditation classes taught at the Dancing Bear Healing Center. It is based on the study of many spiritual disciplines including the Upanishads and Hindu spirituality, Tibetan Buddhism, Hermetic Principals and Egyptian spirituality, Hawaiian Huna spirituality, Celtic spirituality, Native American spirituality, core shamanic spirituality, the Kabbalah, Christian mysticism, and current metaphysical wisdom.

The classes are taught in a format based on the elements of water, air, fire, and earth (steps 1-4 of the 7 steps to enlightenment). The different types of meditation are interspersed into each of the four classes. Many of the class exercises are included within this text. Added to this edition is the fifth element of Ether. The 6ᵗʰ and 7ᵗʰ steps are Ascension followed by Rest which will be expanded on in a later book.

People frequently contact Dancing Bear looking for ways to begin or to advance their meditation practices. It is the intention of this book that your spiritual path be enhanced, and your basic mediation questions are answered. Additionally, once read, anyone will be able to understand the various types of meditation styles available, as well as when and how to use each type of meditation.

Dancing Bear wishes that each reader's spiritual path to enlightenment is strengthened and that you attain total inner peace in this life, now.

Preface to 1ˢᵗ Edition

This book is based on the class material developed for the meditation classes taught at the Dancing Bear Alternative Healing Center. It is based on the study of many spiritual disciplines including the Upanishads and Hindu spirituality, Tibetan Buddhism, Egyptian spirituality, Hawaiian Huna spirituality, Celtic spirituality, Native American spirituality, core shamanic spirituality, the Kabbalah, Christian mysticism and current metaphysical wisdom.

The classes are taught in a four-fold format based on the elements of earth, water, air, and fire. The different types of meditation are interspersed into each of the four classes. For the purposes of this text the format has been changed to be topical in its organization. This will enable the reader to use the book as both a learning tool and as a reference. Many of the class exercises are included within this text.

Tapes of the workshops are also available as well as a separate tape that has two of the primary guided meditations that are used in the classes and referenced in this book.

Many people contact Dancing Bear every week asking how to get started with meditation, or how to get restarted with their previous practice, and many other similar questions. It is hoped that the use of this book will enable to get their answers to these questions and more when they are not able to take the class. That anyone will be able to understand what the various types of meditation are that are available to everyone as well as when and how to use each type of meditation.

It is also hoped that each of you will be helped on your path to enlightenment and that you attain total inner peace in this life, now.

Acknowledgements To 2nd Edition

Special thanks to the many people who have attended meditation workshops and group meditations over the years as well as my spirit helpers, particularly Archangel Metatron for their support, without whom this edition would not be possible.

Special thanks also to the many teachers who have enhanced my life through their teachings, commitments, and love.

Acknowledgements To 1ˢᵗ Edition

It is with much gratitude that I thank the participants of the Meditation workshops for their feedback, making this book possible. Also, special thanks to Catherine Kitcho who has shown me that anything is possible and for editing this manuscript. Great love and thanks to my beautiful and supportive daughter Kristine. Thanks also to all the teachers in my life, some through personal friendship, some from classes, and some by reading their books. It would be impossible to list all the teachers who have helped me here but the bibliography at the end of this book is a good head start. Each book has in some way influenced my life.

A very special thank you needs to go the all the interdimensional beings like angels, spirit teachers, and power animals who have helped me transform and heal. Particularly Archangel Metatron who's guiding light was instrumental in completing this book.

Introduction to 2nd Edition

While in my early forties, I experienced a series of several major, life-changing events. My body was ravaged by seemingly uncontrollable stress resulting from the tumultuous emotional world in which I found myself seemingly trapped. My world began to disintegrate as my health failed me. Doctor visit after doctor visit helped to no-avail. After five near-death experiences and being rushed to the emergency room several times a week I knew something had to change or I would soon die. Then one day a brilliant doctor suggested I try meditation. The word meditation was familiar since I had lived through the sixties but what it meant and where to begin was a mystery to me. I was living the life of an atheist. I had given up spirituality and religion during my youth and had never really looked back at it. Metaphysics seemed a little far out for the straight and narrow left brained person I had grown to be. After all I was an atheist and did not believe in anything spiritual or metaphysical. In a moment of desperation, I realized that I had already tried everything else, why not meditation?

Somewhere from the depths of my memory bank the word TM (Transcendental Meditation) came forward. I associated TM with meditation. So, I began my immersion into the world of meditation looking for people who had any knowledge of TM. A friend shared a book on TM, showing me the basic teachings and meditation style. The process seemed harmless, so I decided to go to my local TM center, not quite knowing what to expect, and inquired about meditation. It was such a challenge to walk into the center that I had to bring a friend just for the emotional support. Stepping through the doors of the center, I was unaware and very naive about the journey and major life transition I was about to make. Thus, began-a journey that would change my life forever.

In March of 1993, I meditated for the first time. As I began meditating my craving for understanding the origins and history of meditation grew like a hunger. I started with the Bhagavad-Gita and the Upanishads, intensely trying to understand the teachings of each. After two months of meditation with TM I "woke up". It was as if I had lived my life in some dream state. The world had shifted. I began to have spontaneous past life memories and discovered that I just knew things. I recalled an event with a friend who had insect bites on the back of her hand that hurt, and I just laid my hand on her bites and they were healed. It all overwhelmed me at first. I was terrified to believe any of this was possible. It went against everything I had believe was true or possible. It was as if a fog was lifted from around me, but I was too afraid to open my eyes and see the world that was right in front of me. Slowly my eyes opened. This was the beginning of what I call my remembering phase.

For the next three years I spent every evening, weekend, and day-off either taking a class, reading a book, or listening to a tape (back then even cars had a tape deck in them). It was as if I was suddenly way behind and needed to catch up, being pushed forward by some invisible force. My path took me to many mystery schools and many traditions. It was during this time that I completed the three-year shamanic study program with the Foundation of Shamanic Studies. Needless to say, I was no longer an atheist and my conversations with the spirit world became the most important part of my day. In the end, I had spent hundreds of hours in formal training in various meditation techniques, thousands hours of formal training in various healing techniques, and over 700 hours of formal training in shamanic practices, all this in addition to the hundreds books on spiritual practices and religious beliefs I had read.

At the end of my three-year remembering journey, I felt as if I had finally reached the point in my education that would enable me to begin my life purpose. People were coming to me and asking for a healing and for psychic readings. My guidance was telling me that I was to change careers, open a healing center, teach classes, and write books. This is the first of many books that are asking to be born. It will not be the last.

The meditation class and ultimately this book came about after a shamanic healing I received from a shaman friend. There is a Buddhist spirit guide that I visit for teaching. When my friend journeyed on my behalf, she was taken to this teacher who presented her with a fragmented soul piece and 22 scrolls. The scrolls were to be studied and a class created for each one. The meditation class and ultimately this book are from the second of the 22 scrolls. A spiritual healing class was developed based on the first scroll.

The first few chapters of this book introduce the concept and importance of meditation followed by meditation techniques grouped by element and describes in detail different meditation as well as when and how to use them. The last chapters are for additional information on spiritual development and personal practices. The appendices contain both a list of books that have been influential in my life as well as web sites on the Internet that contain information of note. Some of the sites are now gone but I leave them in the bibliography for posterity.

In 2002, my journey to be a better healer grew to add acupuncture and herbs to my healing practice and so I moved to another state to attend a medical school there. After school I opened the Dancing Bear Healing Center (a slight change in business name from before I went to school). After 10 years of practice it was clear I needed to begin writing books again and this was my first change. To upgrade this book and republish it with updates. So much more information is now available after over 20 years and the Internet becoming a repository of everything anyone could ever ask about.

May your journey be filled with peace and light, and your heart filled with abundant love.

Peace and Love,

Dancing Bear

1 - What is Meditation?

"Believe those who are seeking the truth; doubt those who find it."
- Novelist Andre Gide

Meditation is often described as a quieting or stilling of the mind. Some say it is an "emptying" of the mind. Since it is impossible to empty the mind it is difficult for many people to understand what they are supposed to do during meditation. This forms the basis of a lot of confusion about meditation since we are not supposed to "do" anything. Some people say, "I try to meditate, but I just cannot". The reason for the challenge is that they "try". It is intended that this book will help you to understand the process of meditation as well as when to use the appropriate technique so that meditation will become simple for you to do. It is further intended that meditation will become an integral part of your everyday life, such that meditation can be practiced as easily and effortlessly as one breathes.

When the mind is quiet, we are able to get in touch with our subconscious mind. Our conscious or rational mind is where we process, analyze, and understand. It is the conscious mind that we seek to still, to quiet, that we ask to step aside for a moment. This allows the subconscious mind to speak. The subconscious mind is the source of our emotions. The subconscious mind is not logical and does not process information, it just senses or perceives. Like Yoda says in "Star Wars" to Luke Skywalker, "feel the force within you".

"When the surface of a lake is still, one can see to the bottom very clearly. This is impossible when the surface is agitated by waves. In the same way, when the mind is still, with no thoughts or desires, you can see the "Self", this is called "Yoga"." - Swami Chidvilasananda

One might wonder why anyone would want to meditate, and this is a good question. Many people associate meditation with eastern religious practices. However, every culture has some sort of meditative practice, all be it with a different name (silent prayer, prayer, a moment of silence, and so on). There have been many studies to assess the benefits of meditation. Some of these benefits are listed below. When you meditate regularly you can expect to benefit in most of these ways:

- Increased peace of mind, a quieting of the "monkey mind"
- You will get to know yourself
- You will become calmer
- Your intuitive capabilities will open up
- Lowered blood pressure
- Reduced heart rate
- Improved ability to concentrate and focus
- Improved grades
- Stronger positive moral values
- Closer connection with nature and Mother Earth
- Increased desire to preserve nature
- You will see more beauty in the world – things will begin to look shiny
- Improved relationships
- No longer taking things personal
- It will be easier to see the Truth that pervades all, i.e., improved discernment
- You will develop a deeper understanding of all that is
- More miracles will begin to come into your life
- You will develop a strong sense of oneness with everything and everyone

Warning: when you meditate you will get to know yourself

It is worth briefly discussing what the brain is doing during meditation. The brain and nervous system are bioelectric and therefore can be electronically measured. When we meditate, we go from the normal waking state of beta into alpha. Some people are able to go into theta. Yogis and long-term meditators can go to a delta state, which is a somnambulistic state. This state is referred to as Samādhi in Sanskrit.

Gamma – a very high vibrational state (40 Hz to 100 Hz)

Beta – normal conscious, waking & thinking state (12 Hz to 40 Hz)

Alpha – light to medium trance (7 Hz to 13 Hz)

Theta – medium to heavy trance (4 Hz to 7 Hz)

Delta – deep trance, body is catatonic except in advanced yogis (<4 Hz)

When you meditate, you are not asleep. The states of sleep, hypnosis, deep prayer, and shamanic journeying are the same states as those of meditation. You are actuality in a heightened state of mental awareness. That does not mean that you will not fall asleep during meditation. Many people complain that every time they try to meditate, they fall asleep. Falling asleep simply means that you are tired and need rest. In that case, sleep is more important than meditation. With today's high stress, fast paced way of life, many people are not getting enough rest, so it is not a problem if you go to sleep, your body obviously needed the time out.

The good news is that if you meditate you may not need as much sleep. It is believed that 20 minutes of meditation is worth one to two hours of sleep. So, if you need more time in your life, you can get it by adding meditation to your daily schedule. Just one hour of meditation is worth a couple hours of sleep. This is why many high energy and very productive people seem to need so little sleep, they meditate.

Meditation is a private practice. When you meditate, at least for the beginner, it is best to find a quiet place where you will not be interrupted by telephones, animals, or people. When you are a seasoned meditator you will be able to meditate anywhere, anytime, and nothing will distract your focus. In the meantime, close the door to your family and turn off the phone, TV, and any other possible distractions.

There are many postures for meditation. The simplest is to just find a comfortable chair where you can sit with your back straight. For most Westerners, this is the easiest posture. If you want to study Yoga and learn about the postures of the various traditions, that is fine, but these postures will not be covered by this text. There are several traditions that practice standing meditation as well as walking meditation, these are great when you are too energetic to sit or very troubled about something.

You might well ask, "who are we that we need to meditate and what does it mean that we will get to know ourselves?" In the Huna tradition it is believed that we have three selves. The middle self, which equates to our conscious self, is that which exists in the arena of space and time. This can be referred to as ordinary reality (OR).

There is the lower self, which is our unconscious mind. It controls all autonomic and bodily functions. The lower self is also the bridge to our higher self, i.e., go down to go up.

Finally, there is the higher self. The higher self is our spiritual self or soul and exists outside of ordinary reality or in what is called Non-Ordinary Reality (NOR). The lower self is the bridge between OR (i.e. middle or conscious self) and NOR (i.e. higher self, soul, or spirit).

When we meditate, we open the communication channels that allow information to flow from NOR to OR. This can be referred to as the Rainbow Bridge. Notice this does not create the flow from OR to NOR. This communication occurs all day long. We are simply are not aware that anyone is sending information until we begin to listen to the messages. No, this is not hearing voices in our head, it is not a schizophrenic state, but a normal state where we hear our soul speaking to us in our own voice and not through our ears. It is a type of telepathic hearing.

2 - Getting Started

There are a few steps that you can take to prepare for meditation. If you are stressed, and your mind is filled with many thoughts, then you might be a bit challenged when you sit down to mediate. In a stressed state one can hardly sit still. This chapter will discuss the mechanics of meditation and give you some exercises that will help prepare you for meditation.

Following are the basic steps to meditation. Each will be explored further in this chapter:

- Prepare your location for meditation
- Ground and center
- Go into a sacred space
- Focus on an anchor
- Come back from the meditation
- Re-ground, center, and wait until completely back in your body.

Preparing a space for meditation may be as simple as closing a door and turning off any electronic or other devices that might interrupt you including any telephones, mobile phones, TV's, etc. Or it may be a ritual that when repeated, tells your body, mind, and spirit that you are about to meditate. Some people have an altar, or just light a candle. Whatever you feel will help you to be calm and relaxed, with no interruptions. It can be simple or elaborate, whatever feels best for you.

Ground means to feel the connection between yourself and the earth. As humans born of the earth, we are connected to "Mother

Earth" or Gaia by an energy force (beyond just gravity). This energy gives us vitality. The Chinese call this Chi or Qi, the Hindu's call the energy Prana, the Japanese call it Ki. When we are connected to the earth, we are physically stronger and mentally more alert. There is also a vibration given off by the earth called the Schuman resonance. When humans ventured into outer space, they discovered that if there was no Schuman resonance (an electromagnetic field of typically 7.83 Hz) that humans did not thrive. As a result, the space station orbiting earth and other manned missions require the Schumann frequency be provided for the astronauts. Must humans operate at 5-10 Hz in the electromagnetic field.

There are many techniques that people use to ground themselves. One common technique is eating. It is recommended that your meditation practice be done prior to eating so that most of your energy is not working on digestion. Fasting is the best state for meditation, especially long meditations. A way to ground without using food is to simply visualize a tube, tree trunk, or other similar object extending from the base of your spine all the way down to the center of the earth. It is also helpful to visualize the tube or tree roots extending from the center of the bottoms of your feet into the center of the earth. Anchor the roots, in the center of the earth and feel earth's energy coming up the tube or roots into your body, filling you with energy. Some perceive this energy as a silver color.

Centering is equally important as it helps stabilize us emotionally and allows energy to flow unblocked throughout our bodies. The easiest way to center is to stand or sit in a position of strength and just sense your center. Tai Chi and similar practices begin with a centering stance. About 2 inches below the bellybutton, inside the body is a structure known as the lower Dantien. It is a major energy center in the body. It is here that one can center. If you prefer you can use your third chakra located just below the Solar Plexus as the point of centering.

In some traditions the practice of spinning is used prior to any spiritual work. It has the effect of centering and grounding you. Always spin in a clockwise direction, arms held out to the sides and even with the shoulders, palms facing down. If you are not used to spinning start out with only a couple of spins. Gradually (over a period of three months) you can add more spins until you reach 21 without falling over or getting dizzy. There is no need to go beyond 21 spins at any given time.

In the Hawaiian Huna tradition they use the "Ha" breath prior to spiritual practice. This practice will ground and center you. It can be used instead of or in addition to the spinning. Stand with your arms down at your sides and slightly extended with your palms facing to the front. Legs should be slightly apart with the toes facing forward, and your back straight. Inhale through your nose, then hold for a count of one, and then exhale through your mouth, making a "Ha" sound, and again hold for a count of one. Do this

HA breath exercise three times. The out breath should be twice as long as the in breath. In other words, if you breathe in for a count of seven, then exhale for a count of fourteen.

Now that you have prepared your space, are grounded and centered, then you are ready to begin meditating. It is time to go into your sacred, or inner space. This has nothing to do with religion. Simply close your eyes and begin to focus inward. When we focus inward, we are going into the realm of our subconscious mind. A place where we can receive messages from our soul. We are leaving the Beta vibration and entering Alpha, or deeper.

There should not be anyone else in your mind with you. This may sound really strange, but if you have ever focused inward and felt as if you were not alone then this is not a strange concept. If you sense anyone else is in your mind with you, then invite them to leave "now"! This is your inner space and yours alone. If you have never experienced these phenomena, there is nothing to be concerned about. If you have experienced this phenomena, then it is time to clear out your mind and energy field. This is called an attachment. If it does not leave, then seek a spiritual healer or shaman to clear out this energy, however, they are only there when you allow them so just your intention should clear them out.

In all meditation practices there is an "anchor". This is the focus of the meditation. Below are listed some of the most well-known types of meditations with their associated anchors:

Classical Meditation Practices:
- **Breath Meditation** – also known as vipassana and prana meditations
- **Mantra Meditation** – use of a word or phrase (never use English, more on this later)
- **Mandala Meditation** – focusing on a circle, special picture, or sacred symbol
- **Chanting** – similar to mantra meditation but contains longer verses, this is a very powerful way to begin any meditation session.
- **Yoga** – Yoga means union of the inner and outer voices, which may be in the form of still or moving yoga. Many in the west think of Yoga as a body fitness exercise but it is so much more than that; yoga is *"between the Jivatman and Paramatman that is between one's individual consciousness and the Universal Consciousness"* - Vishnudevananda Saraswati. Some examples of Yoga include:
  - **Hatha** – Hatha yoga combines postures (called asanas in Sanskrit) with breathing, relaxation, diet and proper thinking. This combination cleanses the body of toxins, clears the mind and brings energy into the total body.

- **Siddha** – Swami Gurumayi Chidvilasananda states that, *"Siddha Yoga meditation is dedicated to the upliftment of humanity and the end of human suffering through the knowledge and experience of the inner Self"*

Other meditation practices:
- **Silent Meditation** or silent prayer – the anchor is the silence
- **Prayer** and affirmations using a sacred language (no English, will talk about this later)
- **Shamanic Journeying** – the process can vary, there are classical or core shamanic practices, cultural practices, as well as any way you create for yourself to journey.
- **Hypnotic Trance** – can be externally induced or self-induced which includes visualizations both externally guided, or internally generated
- **And the list goes on...** any practice that gets one out of Beta and into the calmer vibratory states of being of Alpha, Theta, and Delta.

How to end a meditation session is as important as beginning the practice. Once you have meditated for the allotted amount of time you set aside, then prepare to come back. There are many strategies for coming back effectively. If you just open your eyes and go about your daily business, you run the risk of getting a headache and the meditation will not feel complete. Instead, gently bring yourself back into the room. You can count from one to ten with the intention that you be wide-awake by the number ten. If you were journeying, doing a visualization, or if you had a spontaneous vision it is best to retrace the journey or vision back through every step from the end to the start. This not only helps you to remember the journey but it re integrates your energy preventing soul fragmentation and enabling solid grounding upon return.

Now you can re-ground yourself. This is when a glass of water is helpful. Having a light meal or a handful of nuts may also help you ground. So, if you meditate once in the morning prior to breakfast and once in the evening prior to dinner you can use the meal to re-ground yourself into "ordinary reality".

If when you meditate you become really spacey, and this is not to your liking, then try meditating with your palms face down on your thighs. This helps to stay grounded during the meditation. The Enneagram system categorizes people into three physical types: the head people, the heart people, and the belly people. If you are one of the head people you may experience more challenges in staying grounded than the belly people do. Remember if you feel spacey do not drive or operate any equipment until you are grounded again. It is also helpful to go for a brisk walk after meditating, especially after a long meditation where you came back feeling groggy and tired.

Grounding Exercise

Below is a visualization you can use to ground and center yourself:

1. Close your eyes and visualize the roots of a tree extending from the base of your spine and souls of your feet.
2. Let these roots intertwine with each other and extend to the center of the earth.
3. At the center of the earth visualize a great iron crystal.
4. Imagine your roots winding around the crystal anchoring you there.
5. The earth will send you a silver energy that flows up the roots into your body, filling you with a healing silver energy.
6. Any excess silver energy simply flows back out the roots and down into the earth.
7. Next connect with the sun using your crown chakra
8. The sun will send you a golden energy that flows into the top of your head.
9. This energy flows down through your body.
10. The heart takes the silver earth energy and the golden sun energy and integrates the two then sends them into every cell of your body.
11. Any excess golden energy simply flows back out of your crown chakra and back to the Sun.
12. Allow these energies to ground, center, and energize you.
13. Notice how it feels to be filled with these energies, grounded and centered, now.

3 – Subtle Energy Fields

When studying meditation, it is helpful to understand what is happening from an energy perspective. There are many subtle energy centers and they differ by tradition. That does not mean that one tradition is wrong or better. The energy systems exist concurrently in the same physical space, and some people simply do not perceive the other system. These different traditions have provided names or labels for each energy center. So, for each energy center and system, this reference will use the most commonly known terms, or at least the term that in the opinion of the author, best fits what is experienced. Your experience or beliefs may differ slightly and that is ok.

One might ask, "why is it important for anyone to study energy centers?" The answer is to clear them because they get clogged like the filter to a furnace. Meditation will do this for you. It is also helpful to clear them prior to meditation so that the meditation will clear at deeper levels. The clearing process helps in the creation of a sacred environment, which facilitates the meditation.

From the Hindu tradition comes the notion of chakras. There are seven major chakras on the front of the body with complementary chakras on the back. The exact placement, color, and meaning varies with different traditions and systems as well as the person observing the chakras. Below is one possibility for their colors and meanings.

Chakra Color	Location	Gland	Function/ Meaning
1. RED	root or base	Gonads	vital force energy, passion, Kundalini/safety, security, money
2. ORANGE	sacral	Lymphatic	ambition, sexual energy – emotional/
3. YELLOW	solar plexus	Adrenal	intelligence, mental energy or spleen / control and power
4. GREEN	heart	Thymus	compassion and healing, emotional energy / giving and receiving love
5. LIGHT BLUE	throat	Thyroid	speaking ones truth, teacher, Clairaudient / hearing one's truth
6. INDIGO	third eye	Pineal	all seeing, clairvoyant / seeing one's path
7. PURPLE	crown	Pituitary	all knowing, Claircognizant

Chakras one through three are known as the base chakras. Their source of energy is from the earth. Chakras five through seven are known as the spiritual chakras and their source of energy is the Sun and the cosmos. The heart chakra integrates the energy from the base chakras with the vibrations of the spiritual chakras.

There are other chakras as well, i.e. on the palms of the hands, the souls of the feet, the knees, ear chakras by the temples, one on each shoulder, and others. Their exact location is not important for meditation. The subconscious mind and your soul knows where they are and will clear them for you if you ask.

Prior to any meditation or healing work, it is a good idea to clear your own chakras. There are energy systems that will do this automatically for you or you can just ask that they be cleared prior to meditation. It is also a good idea not to let others work on your chakras. There are very few people who really understand the chakras, which is why there is so much conflicting information. Take responsibility for your own chakras and keep them clear. Once a chakra center gets "blown open", which can happen to the crown chakra with some drugs or gets damaged in some way it is very difficult to heal them or reverse the damage.

So, protect and manage your chakras. There are Solfeggio vibrational music and chants readily available today for clearing and maintaining your chakras.

Chinese medicine is based on the Channel (Vessels) energy system. It has pressure points all over the body with many other connecting energy channels. You do not need to know these points or where the channels are for the purpose of meditation. You only need to know that they exist and the subconscious mind can be used to clear these channels for you just by using your intention. You may even feel the energy moving through these channels as you meditate.

The aura was first studied in the 1700's. In 1939 with the use of Kirlian photography, invented by Semyon Davidovitch Kirlian, it was first scientifically documented in Russia. The body is bioelectric, in other words it is a biological, electromagnetic computer. This energy field emanates out from our body extending anywhere from a few inches to many feet depending on our state of health, emotions, vitality and spiritual development. In most individuals it extends out about three feet. There are seven main layers to the aura. The names differ depending on the system you are using:

- **The Etheric or physical layer**
- **The Astral or emotional layer**
- **The Monastic or mental layer**
- **The Buddhic layer**
- **The Atmic layer**
- **The Monadic layer**
- **The Cosmic layer**

Each of these layers is again subdivided into seven layers. When most psychics do readings for us, they are reading the information we have stored in the layers of our aura. It is not important to be able to see someone's aura, but it is important to know you have one, as well as what you and others are doing with it.

The use of dousing rods is a simple way of seeing how far out your energy field extends. You can make your own rods by bending a coat hanger into two "L" shaped pieces and inserting one end of each rod into their own straw cut in half. Holding the rods inserted into the straw pieces allows the rods to swing easily in your hands. Simply stand about ten feet away from someone and slowly approach him or her with the rods facing them. When you reach their aura the rods will part as if some invisible hand has pushed them apart.

It is important to know your boundaries. This means keeping your aura to yourself. This is easiest to do by prevention. One of the simplest ways to create clear boundaries is to visualize a cylinder of white light around you and ask that any negative energy simply flow down this cylinder into the earth to be recycled. This way we can keep our energy to ourselves and others can keep their energy to themselves. When we are able to do this all day long, we will begin to notice an improvement in our interpersonal relationships and our energy levels will increase. Another option is to visualize yourself in a golden egg of protection. Use which ever method works best for you.

We send out energy cords from our aura and get energy cords sent back to us by others. These energy cords "suck" the energy of the person to whom they are attached. We are not "bad", and others are not bad for sending out cords; we just do not know any better. Now that you know better it is time to prevent cording in your life. To see cords, simply do the following:

- **Rub your hands together**
- **Then touch the tips of your fingers to each other**
- **Slowly move your fingers apart**
- **Stare through the gap in your fingers at a white wall or object behind your fingers**
- **Begin to notice almost clear strands of energy that connect the fingertips**

It is a good daily practice to cut all energy cords. They "suck" the energy of others and in turn others "suck" our energy. It is healthier to keep our energies contained so that we each have a complete energy field with no extrusions or intrusions.

About six inches above the head is an energy field known as the Soul Star. Beneath our feet is another energy center known as the Earth Star. Connecting these two energy centers is what is known as the Central Channel. It is equally important to keep the Central Channel clear because it is our main channel for moving energy between our head to our toes and vice versa. It is akin to the aorta in the blood system - a clogged aorta can be very serious. When our central channel is blocked, we experience problems in our lives that can manifest as serious emotional as well as physical problems. Some may feel this energy movement as Kundalini. My understanding from the masters I have studied with is that once one interferes with the natural flow of this energy through either rituals, or improper practices that is it the most difficult of all aspects on oneself to correct. It is recommended not to do Kundalini practices except with a very experienced and advanced master or teacher or do not do it at all. This energy will rise on its one as one is ready just by meditating on a regular basis. There is no need to force it through other practices. This is the safest way to manage your central channel, just keep it clear.

Within our energy field we store negative thought forms called Samskara in Sanskrit. Even if you do not perceive these thought crystals, it is a good idea to clear them anyway. Have you ever noticed that some people seem to shine more than others do? One of the main reasons is that Samskara creates gray and black energy zones in our auric field. The people around us can feel the Samskara even if they think they are not psychic (everyone is psychic). Most babies are able to clearly see the auras of people, animals, trees, and everything around them. They will play with what they see and smile at the "lights" and may even cry when someone with a lot of dark energy spots comes near them.

Another esoteric aspect of our makeup is that of the seven rays. It is believed that the universe and everything in it is made up of these rays in different combinations. There is the first ray (the source, the origin of all), which splits to form the second ray. The first and second rays combine to form the third ray. These three rays join in combination to form four more rays (rays one and two, rays one and three, rays two and three, and rays one, two and three, an so on) which is the source of the seven rays. It is equally important to keep these rays balanced and harmonized – even if you cannot see, feel, touch, or hear them their high vibration is in everything.

The meaning of the rays follows:

- Ray 1 - Will or Power
- Ray 2 - Love-Wisdom, the ray of God
- Ray 3 - Intelligent Activity
- Ray 4 - Harmony through conflict
- Ray 5 - Concrete Mind and Science
- Ray 6 - Idealism and Devotion
- Ray 7 - Organization and Ritual, Magic, Externalization

Chakra & 7-Ray Systems

7 - Crown Chakra
Violet
Seat of Ketheric Body
Pineal Gland

6 - Brow Chakra
Indigo
Seat of Celestial Body
Pituitary Gland

5 - Throat Chakra
Blue
Seat of Etheric Body
Thyroid Gland

4 - Heart Chakra
Green
Seat of Astral Body
Thymus Gland

3 - Solar Plaxus Chakra
Yellow
Seat of Mental Body
Pancreas Gland

2 - Sacral Chakra
Orange
Seat of Emotional Body
Adrenal Glands

1 - Base Chakra
Red
Seat of Physical Body
Gonads

7-Rays at Each Chakra
7 - Ray 1 Red
6 - Ray 5 Green
5 - Ray 3 Yellow
4 - Ray 2 Blue
3 - Ray 6 Indigo
2 - Ray 7 Violet
1 - Ray 4 Orange

Chart of Chakra System and 7-Rays of God

Excellent reverences for information on the aura, the Central Channel, cords, and the seven rays can be found in the book *The Rainbow Bridge,* by Two Tibetans, many of the Alice Bailey books (see bibliography), as well as *Tapestry of the Gods,* Volumes I & II by Michael Robbins, Ph.D.. *Tapestry of the Gods* is available online in various downloadable formats. Only the first two volumes are relevant.

Another concept that is worth mentioning is the belief in Karma. Karma can be explained by the notion of "what goes around comes around". Because life is an illusion, Karma does not really exist for the spiritually advanced. In the meantime, it is a good idea to clear your Karma and work every day to keep it clear. There are several ways to clear Karma. One is to forgive everyone who has ever hurt you. In the book, *A Course of Miracles,* it discusses forgiveness in great depth. Another way to clear Karma is to transmute it, which everyone can do for themselves. Finally, you can just ask that it be cleared, this method is the easiest to do but the most difficult to achieve if you have not worked on yourself adequately. Meditation helps in this aspect of self-development.

An excellent CD for clearing your energy field is, "I Call Upon All the Angels" produced by Shambhala Vajradhara Maitreya Institute, Inc.

Meditation Exercise

You are going to do a meditation now. Go to a quiet place where you will not be disturbed, sit with your back straight, in a chair, legs uncrossed. If you wish, you can use a small blanket to keep warm. It is risky to lie down while meditating, as it is too easy to fall asleep while in a prone position. Place your feet flat on the floor, no crossing of the legs or feet.

If you like you may perform the spinning and/or Ha breath exercises previously described to ground and center yourself prior to this meditation.

Say the following to yourself:

- **I call on my higher self to ground and center me**
- **I call on my higher self to clear, balance, align, and harmonize my Central Channel**
- **I call on my higher self to clear, balance, align, and harmonize my chakras**
- **I call on my higher self to clear, balance, align, and harmonize my seven rays**
- **I call on my higher self to clear, balance, align, and harmonize the layers of my aura**
- **I call on my higher self to release all cords**
- **I call on my higher self to release undesirable Samskara**
- **I call on my higher self to release unneeded Karma**

Remember clearing karma is not a pass for you to begin doing hurtful actions against others, the earth, animals, plants, Mother Earth, or anything else. It is the beginning of a journey of unconditional love and transformation.

1. Close your eyes and imagine a colored sphere around the first chakra using the color clear red. Release all cords going into or out of this base chakra. Cut any that will not release. Once you have released all cords, then allow the colored energy to fill your entire body. Feel the vibration of the red color in every cell of your body.
2. When you are ready create a sphere around the second chakra using the color orange, clearing the cords and repeating the processes in step one.
3. Continue up the spine in the same fashion until all seven have been cleared with the color that is associated with that chakra in the color system you prefer to use. Release all cords to and from each chakra as you go up your channel.

If you are challenged with this meditation, first record it then play it back to yourself. After several times it will be easier and easier to do until it is second nature. After a while this process just happens automatically every time you sit down to meditate.

If you believe in angels or interdimensional, compassionate beings, you can ask your solar angel or any angel you choose, or being that you like to work with to give you a healing during your meditation and to help you with the clearing work. Archangel Rafael is particularly good with physical healings of all kinds. You may also ask for DNA repair, spiritual upgrades or even downloads. Your spiritual development is up to you, it never hurts to ask for help from above.

4 - Mantra Meditation (Water Element)

Whatever we experience in our internal processing exists only within our own perceptions. When we are able to communicate these internal events and feelings with others, it becomes more real. It exists as a thought form and not just a feeling. The use of language is one way to accomplish this communication. It gives us the foundation for communication, teaching, and personal growth.

All of what humanity thinks and ultimately becomes is determined by the expression of ideas and actions through speech and its derivative, writing. Everything, the Vedas maintain, comes into being through speech. Ideas remain unactualized until they are created through the power of speech. Similarly, The New Testament, Gospel of John, starts "In the beginning was The Word. And the Word was with God and the Word was God..."- Thomas Ashley-Farrand

Mantras are another form of meditation anchor. They bring in the energy of the mantra being chanted. A mantra is "a sound, syllable, word, or group of words that is considered capable of 'creating transformation'" by Feuerstein in *The Deeper Dimension of Yoga*.

Using modern mantras can create unpredictable results since they have not been tested over time or by many people. Using established mantras will create predictable results since they have been used for centuries by many people. Use your inner guidance as to which mantra is best for you.

Many people today are using affirmations in English as meditation anchors. This is not recommended. English is a "contrived" language where the meanings of commonly used words can have the opposite effect on the body than what was intended based on the accepted definition. Sacred languages like Sanskrit, Tibetan, or ancient Hebrew literally vibrate in various parts of the body. Even Mandarin Chinese will vibrate in the body. These vibrations over time heal and elevate that aspect of where they resonate. For example, the Mandarin word for love is "Ai", pronounced like the personal pronounced "I" in English. When used as a mantra it vibrates in the heart and opens it up to more love. But the English word "love" vibrates in the nose and throat. Most Americans speak with a somewhat nasal accent so most English words will vibrate in their nose. Other languages may vibrate in the throat or other part of the body so be aware of this when you select a mantra. The ancient languages vibrate all over the body and have a more musical feel to it. Ancient writings even have a more poetic rhythm to them such as the ancient story *The Epic of Gilgamesh* (see bibliography for a downloadable version). So, find a mantra where you resonate with the meaning and use that if you need a mantra or a chant to meditate with. Keep in mind many advanced meditators use breath meditation with visualizations and proper posture in addition to a mantra or chanting. Sometimes chanting the mantra at the beginning of the meditation is a great way to start then switch to silent meditation and only use the mantra when you notice you have become lost in your thoughts.

Mantra meditation is excellent for healing, transformation, and manifestation. It can be equated to the element of water, which has these same properties. If you learn Transcendental Meditation (TM) a specific mantra is given to you that is usually the name of one of the Hindu deities. The book, *Levitation* by Steve Richards, contains the TM mantras and other information about TM. These mantras work well for inducing trance. If you are challenged by a chatty mind or "monkey mind" then maybe mantra meditation is best for you at this time.

We will next explore some of the better-known mantras in use today and what each of these mantras can do for you.

Om

One of the most well-known and used mantras is Om or Aum. It is referred to as the sound of the universe. "The all-encompassing, the uncreated, the unchanging. The "mind" of the Universe, Original Nature, Buddha", per Darrell McLaughlin in an e-mail. In Buddhism, **Om** is the universal Buddha mind. It is enlightenment or Nirvana. It is simultaneously the source and the destination of everything. From the center, out to all sorts of individualities and then back to the center again.

Simply use "Om" as the anchor for your meditation. The mantra is "rolled" through the mouth such that all the vowel sounds are created followed by the m sound, i.e. a e i o u m. Creating white noise with this mantra can have an uplifting and clearing effect on the environment. A good sound production using this mantra repeated is: "Hypnotic OM" produced by Red Ball On Blue Water.

Below is Om in Sanskrit:

Sanskrit for Om

Om Ah Hum Soha

This mantra functions on many levels, below is a rudimentary explanation:

- **Om, Ah, Hum** represents the three bodies of Buddha.
  - **Om is the universe, the universal, the all-encompassing.**
  - **Ah is the Buddhas and Bodhisattvas (Buddhas to be), such as Shakyamuni Buddha, founder of present day Tibetan Tantric Buddhism. It is the Truth embodied. The Word and "speech" of the Universe or Dharma.**
  - **Hum is the correspondent to Siddhartha Gautama, the human being who became Shakyamuni Buddha. It is the fruition, and refers to physical manifestations, i.e. the "body" of the Universe or Sangha.**
- "**So Ha**" means something like the way Christian's use "amen" to end a prayer. The more literal meaning is "so be it", or "let it be".

Many tantric Buddhist mantras have the format of **"Om Ah Hum … Soha".** It is the wrapper, if you will, for other mantras.

Om Mane Padme Hum

Everything has many levels of meaning – those presented here are only one view. Roughly translated it means salutations to The Jewel of Consciousness (the mind) which has reached the heart's lotus.

- **Om** - seed syllable (see above)
- **Mane Padme** - "Jewel in the Lotus"
- **Hum** (Sanskrit) / **Hung** (Tibetan) - seed syllable (see above)

The Jewel in the Lotus is frequently understood to be a reference to Avalokitesvara, the Bodhisattva of Compassion, known in Tibetan as Chenrezig, and of whom the Dalai Lama is said to be an emanation. Tara is the female manifestation of Avalokitesvara. It is believed that she was created by his tears of compassion.

Mantras in and of themselves do not really have a meaning, in that mantras are inherently untranslatable - they are not like sentences in a foreign language. They are more like a metaphoric teaching in which the meaning of the mantra is only understood through its practice. If you practice the mantra enough you realize its meaning inherently.

"This is not to deny that some of the words may have or have had a meaning in another language, nor that the syllables of the mantra cannot be used to point at meanings and be used as teachings. These things work at many levels." - 'o-Dzin

It is believed that the Om Mane Padme Hum mantra provides protection for your path. Another meaning of this mantra is based on the six realms of the Buddhist tradition:

- **Om**   Buddha
- **Ma**   Bodhisattva
- **ne**   Human
- **Pad**   Animal
- **me**   Hungry ghost
- **Hum**   Demon

"This mantra is practiced more than any other in the world. It is pre-eminent in producing a state of dynamic compassion in the chanter. Dynamic means that this compassion contains as part of it the ability to powerfully manifest in both subtle and obvious ways. One of the simple yet profound teachings which can be gained by using this mantra is the concept that when the mind and heart become united, anything is possible. The implications of this simple notion are staggering. If you want to change the world for the better, this mantra should be in your spiritual toolbox." - Thomas Ashley-Farrand

A musical version of this mantra is, "I Call Upon All the Angels" produced by Shambhala Vajradhara Maitreya Institute, Inc.

Om Namaha Shivaya

This mantra has no approximate translation. The sounds relate directly to the principles which govern each of the first six chakras on the spine and the elements of earth, water, fire, air, and ether. Notice that this does not refer to the chakras themselves, which have a different set of seed sounds, but rather the principles which govern those chakras in their place.

"A very rough, non-literal translation could be something like, 'Om and salutations to that which I am capable of becoming.' This mantra will start one out on the path of subtle development of spiritual attainments. It is the beginning on the path of Siddha Yoga, or the Yoga of Perfection of the Divine Vehicle." - Thomas Ashley-Farrand

A musical version of this chant is "Om Namaha Shivaya" produced by Spring Hill Music.

Om Tare Tuttare Ture Soha

This mantra is not as well-known but since this book was originally dedicated to Tara, her mantra is included. Specifically, this is the Green Tara (Harit हरित in Hindi or Dolma in Tibetan) one of the manifestations of the 14 known emanations of Tara. There are many Thangkas or Tankas with the 14 emanations of the Taras. Others say there are more, up to 21 emanations. There is no known meaning that this author could find. One possible meaning is "To you, embodiment of all the Buddhas' actions, I prostrate always — whether I am in happy or unhappy circumstances — with my body, speech and mind." According to the YoWangdu Experience Tibet web site (www.YoWangdu.com).

The practice of this chant brings in for the author an immediate higher connection with spirit, a sense of awakening and expansion. It seems to clear the energy field and then bring in a tremendous amount of vital life force energy. Tara connects us with our feminine side creating an opening of the heart and expansion of compassion within us.

This mantra is invigorating and can easily be danced to as well as chanted.

A great recording of the Green Tara mantra can be found at: www.youtube.com/watch?v=eBopONbgNpQ.

So Hong

This is a waking mantra and is great for reducing stress when closing your eyes is not appropriate or difficult to do. You can use this mantra when driving, in meetings or other times when you need to center but do not want to risk "getting spaced out". This mantra is from Dan Millman.

Meditation Exercise:

Do each of the above mantra meditations 1,000 times each. After each meditation write in a journal how you are feeling and what you experienced. You will know if any of these mantras are good for you at the very least. You will also better understand what each mantra can do for you.

If you get really good at using these mantras you can chant the mantra in the back of your mind all day long, Om Mane Padme Hum is really good for this but you may prefer a different mantra. Your day will be much brighter, and you will find it impossible to get angry if you do silent chanting all day long, or as much as possible. One of my past teachers, Master Samantha of the True Buddha School recommends chanting Om Mane Padme Hum one-million times. It is also the mantra used when doing Kora around a Stupa and is printed on all Buddhist flags that are hung so that they blow in the wind sending peace and love to the earth and all of humanity.

5 - Breath Meditation (Air Element)

Breath meditation focuses on the element of air and breath, movement and the senses. The breath (Prana in Hindu, Ha in Hawaiian, Ra in Egyptian) is used as the anchor for meditation. When we are stressed our breath is shallow and can be rapid. To meditate we need to be calm. When we breathe in slow deep breaths, we change our entire energy field, emotions, vibration, as well as our state of mind. As a result, we become open to the spiritual aspect of our being.

The "in breath" is symbolic of receiving while the "out breath" is symbolic of giving.

To meditate using the breath, simply notice the breath. With experience, you will begin to notice that you breathe with your heart, and eventually with all of your chakras, as well as through all the pores in your skin. This expanded awareness need not be focused on. It will just happen naturally over time.

Breath meditation is the beginning exercise in learning Vipassana meditation. Once the breath is mastered, which for some could take a lifetime, then other aspects are noticed. A new aspect is added as a focus of meditation only once its predecessor is mastered. Other anchors might be body sensations, the heartbeat, thoughts, and so on. If you want to learn Vipassana or any advanced breath meditation it is best to find a master to study with who can guide you. This is a very spiritual meditative practice when done properly.

If you wish, you can learn to "manage" your breath. This means to consciously breathe. Breathe in and count, hold for a count of one, then exhale for double the counts of the in breath, hold for a count of one, then repeat. You might start with a count of seven for the in breath and fourteen for the exhale or out breath. Over time, this count can be increased. Increase the count only as much as you are able to without disrupting the rhythm or becoming out of breath. You should be able to master this to the point that you just notice the breath as the anchor and not make the counting the anchor.

An excellent book for more information on breath meditation is *Wherever You Go There You Are - Mindfulness Meditation in Everyday Life* by Jon Kabat-Zinn.

Kidney Breath Exercise and Meditation

This next exercise will change your energy, so practice it carefully.

- Go to your internal special place and ground
- Light a candle, setting the intention that you will now meditate as you ignite it or perform whatever meditation ritual you have created for yourself.
- Set the intention of your meditation (inner peace, knowledge, healing, etc.)
- Place your hands on your lower back over the kidneys and breathe deeply three times noticing that the kidney area expands. If it does not expand, then you are not breathing deeply enough. If you are not able to comfortable place you hands on your kidneys then place them on your lower abdomen.
- Begin to breathe slowly
- Once your hands move out with each breath you may place them on your lap
- Say a prayer to set intention for the time of the meditation (i.e. "I wish my mind to quiet now for the next 20 minutes")
- Enter your internal, sacred space
- Notice the in breath
- Notice the out breath
- If you have a thought, simply notice the thought and return to the breath anchor
- After 20 minutes – very slowly come back into the room
- Re-ground yourself

Remember that when you come back too quickly from a meditation or do not ground yourself afterwards, you run the risk of getting a headache, becoming cranky, and feeling spaced out. Give yourself time and space. If you only have twenty minutes to meditate, then only go into your inner space for ten to fifteen minutes to allow yourself time to come back. If you are willing to make the time it is better to meditate for a minimum of twenty minutes and allow five to ten minutes to come back. This is akin to the cool down period after a heavy workout.

Meditation is about slowing down and going within – not going to sleep, mentally you will be in a heightened state of awareness.

6 - Meditation with Prayer (Fire Element)

Silent Prayer

Silent prayer and other forms of Meditation - focus on the element of fire, digestion and the creation and maintenance of the body. Silent prayer simply makes silence the anchor for the meditation. This is a good practice for learning to quiet the conscious mind since the silence or "unthought" is the anchor.

Prayer with Words

Prayer with words can be used for many purposes including healing, spiritual development, and manifestation. One of the most profound prayer formats I have ever experienced is the one taught by Irving Feurst, Founder of the Spiritual Unfoldment Network. The format follows:

For myself I ask for …, …, …, …
For my family I ask for …, …, …, …
For my friends I ask for …, …, …, …
For the people of <any city> I ask for …, …, …, …
For the people of <any state or province> I ask for …, …, …, …
For the people of <any country> I ask for …, …, …, …
For the people of <any hemisphere> I ask for …, …, …, …
For the people of the earth I ask for …, …, …, …
For the beasts and animals, I ask for …, …, …, …
For the trees and plants, I ask for …, …, …, …
For the minerals I ask for …, …, …, …
For the … I ask for …, …, …, …

Where …, …, …, … is anywhere from one to as many objects as you can remember to request at one time. It is best to visualize the object you are asking about (i.e. the people of the earth) as well as the object you are asking for (i.e. peace, love, harmony, good health, abundance, …). The prayer can be shortened or lengthened by changing the objects/people for which/whom you are asking.

A simple example of this prayer might be:

> For myself I ask for enlightenment
> For the people of the earth I ask for enlightenment
> For the animals and beasts, I ask for enlightenment.

The challenge with this prayer is to stay grounded enough to not get lost in it.

Prayer was something that for many years I felt I just could not master. Others always seemed to have great prayers and I felt mine were lacking. Then I took a Celtic Shamanism workshop from Dr. Tom Cowan and this changed forever. Celtic prayers are so easy to create, and their impact can be profound.

To create a Celtic prayer simply go into a meditative state (your inner space) and think of the purpose of your prayer. Then note the first thing that comes to your mind. It might be the sun, the moon, an animal, the weather, or a feeling, anything at all. Then ask this thing in your mind what is its gift. Each line of the prayer is the "thing" followed by its gift. The language can be creative – it does not have to follow normal rules of grammar so let yourself go. In fact, if you deviate from normal language the prayer seems to be more powerful so have fun with it.

Over the years I have written and collected many such prayers and here share some of them with you as well as other prayers:

> All the blessings of the earth for your New Year
> All the blessings of the sun for your New Year
> All the blessings of the moon for your New Year
> All the blessings of the stars for your New Year
> All the blessings of the animals for your New Year
> All the blessings of the plants for your New Year
> All the blessings of the wind for your New Year
> All the blessings of the spirits for your New Year
> All the blessings for your New Year
> Unknown

I wish you joy and prosperity with all my heart
I wish you joy and prosperity with all my voice
I wish you joy and prosperity with all my soul
I wish you joy and prosperity with all my mind
I wish you joy and prosperity with all my attention
I wish you joy and prosperity with all my being
I wish you joy and prosperity
Unknown

May the peace of a golden sunset bless your path
May the joy of a newborn bless your days
May the light of the moon caress your nights
May the strength of Bear be with you always
Dancing Bear

May the azure of blue lift you
May the subtle light of moon guide you
May the softness of water caress you
May the spirit of oneness be in you
May the joy of Great Spirit be with you always
Dancing Bear

May the winds of change blow gently upon you
May the rays of the sun warm your day
May the light of moon guide you through the darkness
May the strength of Bear give you courage
May the grace of the Divine be on you always
Dancing Bear

May the warmth of the sun light your days
May the power of Pele warm your heart

May the subtle light of moon light your nights
May the ribbit of a frog guide your thoughts
May the gentleness of deer guide your heart
May Mother earth hold you in her womb
May the awe of great spirit be with you always.
Dancing Bear

Namaste'
I honor the place in you, in which the entire universe dwells
I honor the place in you, which is of love, of truth, of light, and of peace
When you are in this place in you and I am in that place in me,
We are One.

Meditation Exercise:

In a journal write a prayer. Just allow the prayer to flow from your heart into your hand. If you get images then either draw or write the first image that comes to mind, no analysis. If you hear sounds, then write what that sound represents. If you feel or sense "things" then write the name of the object that you feel or sense. Then ask what the gift is that this object brings and write that down. Continue this until a closing phrase appears or it just becomes obvious that there are no more images, sounds, or feelings. Read back what you have written to yourself a couple of times. Then just do a simple breath meditation and see what comes up for you.

After your meditation write about what you received during the meditation in your journal.

7 – Other Meditations

Mandalas

Mandalas are any design that is focused on as the anchor of a meditation. Celtic shamans initiate their journey by going through an intricate maze. The Hopi and Tibetans use sand mandalas for meditation, healing, and manifestation. Stained glass windows in cathedrals are also a form of mandala.

The Native American dream catcher is a form of mandala. The elder shaman would create one for his/her apprentice. If the elder shaman should die before the apprentice had completed his/her training, then the apprentice could simply journey through the hole in the center of the dream catcher to the elder shaman's spirit and complete their training.

Drawing mandalas can be very therapeutic. Simply draw (crayons or watercolors work great for this) whatever your hand wants (if you are blocked simply use your non-dominant hand and put your inner critic mind to bed). Then meditate on the drawing.

Sacred Symbols

Volumes of information describing sacred symbols and sacred geometry exist. Their meanings can be varied depending on the culture that values them. The real meaning of all symbols, however, is what you give it. This is important to remember when doing healing work and interpreting dreams for others. Each person gives each symbol its meaning and not anyone else. For example, a snake may be a fearful animal to one person and a great healing spirit to another person.

If you are attracted to a specific symbol you may simply meditate on it. It becomes your anchor. Allow the symbol to speak to you. You can use any of the traditional symbols, Reiki symbols, shapes, oracle cards, whatever you are curious about understanding. In sacred geometry the Star Tetrahedron is considered by some to be the "seed of the universe". The primary shapes that are considered sacred: triangle, circle, sphere, square, cube, rectangle, pyramid, star tetrahedron, five-pointed star or pentagram, and others.

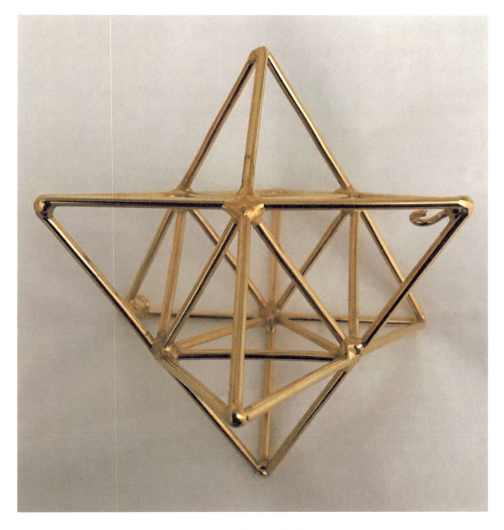

Sacred Symbols

Letters of the alphabet are also considered sacred symbols. The spiritual meaning of letters has been lost in the everyday consciousness of most people. In the Kabbalah it is possible to uncover some of the spiritual meaning of our Arabic alphabet. Simply meditate on an individual letter to understand it. It is important to understand the first letter of your birth name. It is what you have come into this world to learn. In the book *Change Your Handwriting, Change Your Life* by Vimala Rodgers she talks about letters and their meaning.

Numbers also have sacred meaning. Numerology, the study of the sacred meaning of numbers and how they affect our lives, is a very old science where each number has its own value and meaning. Every aspect of our being can be calculated down to eleven numbers (1 through 9, 11, and 22). Knowing your life path number, soul number, personality number, and karmic lessons can help facilitate your spiritual growth. The best way to know your numbers is to get a book on Numerology and calculate your numbers. Then meditate on your numbers to understand why they are important for you in this life.

Gematria is another numbering system that is very powerful in understanding the meaning of words, places, dates and so forth. Know what your birth name means in the different systems as this is part of who you are and why your soul incarnated into this life with your current aspects.

Moving Meditation

Moving meditation is any movement done with purpose. All the martial arts, all the various Yoga practices, many types of dancing (i.e. Hula, Tantric Dance, Belly Dancing, etc.), Tai Chi, Chi Gong, and many more are examples of moving meditation. I have even heard of people riding their bike as a means of doing moving meditation. The advantage of moving meditation is its ability to help bring the mind and body together as one.

A simple moving meditation is to just stand erect, stare straight ahead, and gently sway back and forth. Another simple moving meditation is to put on some perky music that you enjoy. Close your eyes and just start moving. Be sure to remove all breakables from the room until you have mastered the art of moving without bumping into things. This will teach you to see with your eyes closed.

Shamanic Meditation

Shamanic journeying is as old as mankind. The word shaman comes from Siberia. Anthropologists use the term to mean the spiritual healer in indigenous cultures. There are many names for shaman in other cultures, like Kahuna in Hawaiian.

In some cultures, like Cherokee, they have Medicine men/women. This is not the same as a shaman. Medicine men/women do not journey in the same way, they may function more in a healing and religious capacity or as specialists like in makers of tools. In this tradition the shaman usually lives apart from the tribe while the Medicine men/women are an integral part of the tribe. They may have specialties besides healing like weaving, beading, arrow making, and so on. In indigenous peoples of South America like in the Amazon area, the shaman is the medicine man/woman, there is no separation of function.

Today there are several types of journeying available to us, i.e. classical, cultural, and modern. By classical I simply mean to listen to a rapid drumbeat. Some cultural types of journeying include listening to a Didgeridoo, using a rattle, a bell, or using anything that makes a sound that can be used as an anchor. Modern journeying might include electronically generated music or any repetitive sound from a modern device.

The difference between journeying and other meditations is that there is a specific purpose for the meditation, the person on the journey will visit a specific spirit (animal or teacher) and will follow a known path.

The easiest way to learn this meditation is to use Michael Harner's book, *The Way of the Shaman*, or to take a weekend workshop from the Foundation of Shamanic Studies (http://www.shamanism.org/) or other shamanic teacher..

The use of shamanic journeying is one of the most profound ways to develop a spiritual connection, receive guidance, and to help others. However, this path is not for everyone. Meditate on the idea of shamanism first and see if it is for you. If not, then meditate with angels or other spirit teachers, whatever fits in your belief system and feels comfortable to you. Just remember that whatever path you take that there is always a bit of a struggle in the beginning as you practice. Give yourself time without any judgments to learn.

Meditation with Hypnosis

The hypnotic state and the meditative state are one and the same. All hypnosis is self-hypnosis. Some people tell me they do not meditate but use self-hypnosis. If the word meditation pushes buttons for you then simply substitute the term hypnosis for meditation.

There are two primary ways to enter into an hypnotic trance. You can use an internal or an external induction. Internal is one that you create yourself and just think. External is one that someone says aloud to you or that you listen to from a recording, these are also referred to as guided visualizations. Less specific ways to induce trance is to listen to music, i.e. chanting, Bach, metaphysical music, Didgeridoo music, etc.

Last but not least, the easiest way to go into a hypnotic trance is to drive home after a very stressful day at the office. If you have ever wondered how you got home after driving, then you know what a hypnotic trance is firsthand. While this is not recommended, I include it to demonstrate how easy it is to go into trance. We do it, all the time, every day; while watching TV, reading a book, or listening to someone we really do not want to hear.

Meditating with Crystals

Crystals are programmable, can be cleared, and can be personalized for you. This is a good thing to do prior to meditating with the crystal. There are many books and theories on how to clear crystals and I have tried them all. In the end it is my experience that all of the clearing and programming can be done just by holding the crystal in your dominant hand (both hands for larger crystals) and simply intending that they be cleared and personalized. In other words, you clear the crystal by your intention by placing your attention on the crystal.

Other uses of crystals are to clear a room, remove thought forms, use for protection, and cutting cords. By meditating with the crystal you will be able to communicate with the crystal. First look at the crystal and feel it in your hand. Then do a simple breath meditation. Information from the crystal will flow into you in whatever way you receive information best; i.e., clairvoyantly (internal knowing usually with the third eye), clairaudiently (hearing), clairsentiently (knowing by feeling or sensing), or claircognizantly (just knowing including the future). Stones and crystals are very old and very wise. There is much to be learned from them. Some crystals like <u>clear</u> quartz crystals (the male crystals) are very good at enhancing meditation and are easily programmed for desired affects. <u>Milky</u> quartz crystals (female crystals) are very good at enhancing dreams (simply place it under your pillow at night and meditating on it in the morning to remember your dreams).

Subtle Energy Meditations

Subtle or esoteric energies have been around and used for healing for as long as mankind has been around. Jesus used them for healing in the Bible. The most widely used subtle energy known in the United States today is Reiki. There are many hundreds of subtle energies from all over the world. Some energies, like Reiki, require an empowerment (or attunement, or Shakti) in order to run the specific energy frequency. These empowerments are passed down through a specific lineage. Other energies do not require empowerments, such as color energies, vibrational energies, and the like. Energies can also be channeled in by anyone who is connected with their higher self and asks for it to come through to them. They can also be remembered from past lives. Once you have an empowerment you have it for all time and future lives.

Meditating with subtle energies does many things for us. It strengthens the body's ability to channel the energy through us and clears our channels by removing blockages. This is especially helpful if you are using the energies for healing work. Meditating with the energy also opens us up to understanding the energy and its uses better. The energy will begin to communicate with us in a knowing way. Subtle energies heal us, increase our vibration, and restructure our energy field to varying degrees depending on the energy system being used. Anyone who uses any subtle energy in their personal life on themselves or on others will benefit from meditating with that energy. Just keep in mind that people heal themselves, we are only the healing facilitator. Unless you are a very advanced healing facilitator it is best to allow the persons own soul to determine which energy frequency they need for their highest good at that moment in time. Otherwise, you run the risk of giving them your karma and illnesses as well as taking the other persons karma and illness. I can not count how man times people have come to me either because someone "gave them a healing" and now they are sick or feel out of sorts, or they gave a healing and are now having issues or health concerns in their life.

To do the meditation with crystals, gems, or stones simply go into your inner space and begin to channel the energy. It is usually best to have your palms down on your thighs when doing energy meditation so that the energy will fill the body, flow out of the hands and then back into the body. It is important to be very grounded when doing energy meditations so that the excess energy will flow out through the feet into the earth as well as back out of the crown of your head (seventh chakra).

Some subtle energies flow better when accompanied with visualization. For Reiki, either the symbols can be visualized, or the color violet can be visualized. If visualization is not your strength, then have a picture of a symbol to look at first or something that is violet colored (like a crayon or scarf). For Egyptian energies visualizing an Ankh may help, for Tibetan energies where there is no symbol, then the symbol of Om in Sanskrit or the color of the energy can be used. For most subtle energies the color of the energy is all that is needed. Some energy meditations have specific symbols that are to be visualized. You will need to find out from someone in that lineage which symbol is best to use.

Egyptian Ankh

Below is Reiki in Japanese as well as the "Reiki Ideals" from Mrs. Takata. Reading the ideals prior to meditating with Reiki can help to bring one into a contemplative state prior to meditating.

Reiki in Japanese

Reiki Ideals

Just for today, I will let go of anger.
Just for today, I will let go of worry.
Just for today, I will give thanks for my many
blessings.
Just for today, I will do my work honestly.
Just for today, I will be kind to my
eighbor and every living thing.

Mrs. Takata, Reiki Master

8 - Communicating with Spirit Teachers (Earth Element)

When you forgive, you open your heart to love which makes room in your life for angels
-Archangel Rafael

Angels

It seems that today in the United States there is a revival of communicating with angels. I'm not sure when we stopped communicating with angels, but it has been my personal experience that this is one of the most profound ways of receiving personal and spiritual guidance, facilitating the healing of others, and enriching my life. The amazing thing is that angels are always there for us and there is an angel for everything. It does not matter who you are, you may call on any angel or archangel at any time and they just show up. The challenge is to learn to hear them. They always hear us. No prayer goes unanswered – we may not always appreciate the answer, but the prayer is always heard and answered in the way that is best for our highest good.

One simple way to communicate with angels is to start with your own solar or guardian angel. EVERYONE has a personal solar angel, yes, even you. Simply meditate with the intention that the communication between you and your angel be enhanced. Begin by asking yes and no questions where you already know the answer. It is helpful to ask questions where the answer is obviously wrong. Then just notice how the answer is received by you. The experience will vary for different people, there is no one answer nor is there a right or wrong answer. The answer will be the best way for you to receive the message. Once you know how your angel will communicate with you then ask your angel to "turn up the volume". Make sounds louder, feelings stronger, images brighter and clearer, or knowing more profound – however you get your information ask that it be intensified. Practice, practice, practice … until you can easily and effortlessly communicate with your angel. Keep in mind that angels are interdimensional beings, you may not see them as beings with wings but as animals, totems, or even as imaginary beings. Whatever form they use to appear to you is ok.

Before communicating with your angel, it is always a good idea to test with a few yes/no questions and then always ask if your ego is responding or if the information is really coming from your angel. Sometimes the answer will be that the information is coming from your ego. When this happens to me, I know I need to meditate more to clear my ego's interference. It is okay when the ego interferes, that is what egos do, it is only important to be aware of the possibility of the ego's interference, and to keep your ego from modifying or creating the information that you receive. Being humble helps to mitigate this aspect of the ego interference.

Angels, in return for their help appreciate gratitude. We learned as children to say thank you whenever we are given a gift. This applies to the angels as well. It's a good habit to always thank them for their help. Although they do forgive us when we forget to thank them, compassionate beings that they are, it is still good form. Gratitude is an essential part of any spiritual practice.

By working with your angel, we can understand your soul purpose and know which path will be the best one for you to take. When your emotions (subconscious self) and thoughts (conscious self) are not in synch, then we have challenges manifesting in the material world. Communicating with our angels helps to get our inner self (unconscious mind) and our outer self (conscious mind) on the same path.

For more information on angels Dr. Doreen Virtue has several books and tapes that are excellent references.

Spirit Teachers and Spirit Animals

For centuries humans have communicated with spirit teachers and spirit (power) animals. They educate us, heal us, guide us, comfort us, and love us. They help us heal others, defend ourselves, and many more things just like angels do. Communication with spirit teachers and animals can be done the same way as with the angels. It is also very helpful to merge with the spirit teacher or animal. Simply visualize the teacher or animal in front of you and then have it merge with you. Your energy field will change, and you will become one with the teacher or animal. This is known as shape shifting and is commonly practiced by most shamans.

9 – Rainbow Body (Ether Element)

Many people eventually advance to the point of achieving an almost magical advanced spiritual state and vibration. This is possible in many traditions; the Tibetan Buddhist have well documented examples of meditators who transformed themselves into light either upon their death or as they left their bodies if they decided to leave the earth plane voluntarily. Jesus ascension into heaven might be considered his transition into rainbow light.

> Often masters that attain the Rainbow body will return one last time out of compassion for their beloved disciples and give what are known as posthumous teachings, delivered in the form of a last testament. Often the master is in the transfigured state on occasion suspended in the sky.

From: https://soonyata.home.xs4all.nl/sorubasamadhi.htm

Padmasambhava is a well-known Buddha that lived in around the 8th century and achieved a rainbow body. His tangka is below showing him in his rainbow body form.

When you came into this world, you came without a single investment. So whatever happens in your life, anyway you are in profit.
-Sadhguru

Padmasambhava Rainbow Body Tangka

There are several books as well as online classes in how to achieve the Rainbow body. Once you have become an experienced meditator and worked on yourself sufficiently then this will be the most advanced process you can undertake to continue your spiritual journey.

This process is not for the faint of heart. It is challenging and difficult. You must be able to transform your beliefs, attitudes, thinking, as well as be willing to dedicate a great deal of time to your spiritual development. In Tibetan Buddhism it is known as Dzogchen. The mandala to meditate on shows a special symbol. This may have a rainbow around it.

Dzogchen Mandala

Below is the Dzogchen Mantra to chant while looking at the image:
"Tayata Om
Bekandze Bekandze
Maha Bekandze
Radza Samudgate Soha"
Source: www.youtube.com/watch?v=wIZqghmN24U

In English it says;

> May the many sentient beings who are sick, quickly be freed from sickness. And all the sicknesses of beings Never arise again. - Mahakatha meditation mantras and music.

So, what is Dzogchen exactly?

> "Dzogchen (Wylie: rdzogs chen) or "Great Perfection", Sanskrit: अति योग, is a tradition of teachings in Tibetan Buddhism aimed at discovering and continuing in the natural primordial state of being. It is a central teaching of the Nyingma school of Tibetan Buddhism and of Bon. In these traditions, Dzogchen is the highest and most definitive path of the nine vehicles to liberation."

Source https://en.wikipedia.org/wiki/Dzogchen

At www.Dzogchen.org they say that "*Dzogchen is an enlightening practice, a universal wisdom tradition, and a spiritual community.*"

This type of meditation involves your posture, chanting, visualization, and thoughts all at the same time. There is a sect of Zen Buddhists as well as other Buddhists that teach this method of transformation. It is too complex to describe here in any further detail. This is serves only as a brief introduction to this very advanced meditation and transformation process.

Developing the Rainbow Body

> A life without love is a waste, "should I look for spiritual love, or material, or physical love?", don't ask yourself this question. Discrimination leads to discrimination. Love doesn't need any name, category or definition. Love is a world itself. Either you are in, at the center... either you are out, yearning.   - Rumi

Recommended resources include:
- *Quintessential Dzogchen* by Erik KunDema Kunsang & Marcia Binder Schmidt
- *Rainbow Painting* by Tulku Urgyen Rinpoche
- https://soonyata.home.xs4all.nl/sorubasamadhi.htm

10 - What's Next?

Building an Altar

Creating an altar enhances the intention to meditate. By creating a sacred space with sacred objects which you hold as most sacred to you, will help you to meditate. The altar can be as simple as a few stones or crystals laid out on a piece of cloth. Add a candle and some incense or sage and you have an altar.

Ask spirit to bless the altar and then meditate. Fresh cut flowers are nice to add to the altar. Bottled water can be left next to the altar with the intention that the spirits bless the water. The water can later be drunk (sipped) to help you cleanse, heal, or just feel better.

The purpose of the candle is to represent spiritual connection through the rising smoke. It also adds to the ritual of beginning meditation, simply light the candle on the altar with the intention to meditate.

After lighting the candle and incense, set the boundaries of the sacred space. In Buddhism this means setting the Dharma boundaries, in Celtic and Native American traditions they honor the four directions. This helps to create a protective energy field around your sacred space, protecting it from negative energy.

Rituals and Spiritual Practices

Rituals and spiritual practice help us to communicate with our subconscious mind and ultimately, the spirit world. If every time you begin a particular practice you do the same things (like lighting a candle) your subconscious mind learns and just knows to pay particular attention to your intentions and that it will be expected to retrieve messages for you from the spirit realm.

Potpourri

Thoughts are very powerful. Most people have no idea just how much damage they can do to themselves and others with negative thought forms. Negative thoughts actually form thought crystals, which get stored in our aura or energy field as dark spots. Thought forms can be used to manipulate and hurt others as well as ourselves. Meditation will help us to have positive thoughts throughout the day. Keeping a cylinder of white light around us at all times will help prevent the negative thoughts of others from entering our energy field.

It is important to develop a meditation practice. Like exercise, a regular habit improves its effectiveness. That said, a good meditation is any meditation that you do. It is cumulative throughout all your lifetimes. The more regular your meditations, however, the more you will experience its benefits in this lifetime.

A good way to get started is to meditate twenty minutes every day (first thing in the morning or in the evening). If you only have ten minutes one day that is okay but try to do the meditation every day at the same time. It is important to develop a habit. Meditate prior to eating and not on a full stomach. After you feel that you have a good habit developed then begin meditating twice a day for twenty minutes.

After a while (anywhere from two months to two years) you will begin to know that your meditations need to be longer. You will know when this happens. Add five minutes to the morning meditation and take five minutes away from the evening meditation. As you become comfortable with the longer meditation then add another five minutes. Do this until you have one forty-minute to one-hour meditation per day.

Once you are meditating for at least forty minutes a day it is very important that you be very regular with your practice. Otherwise, you will need to go back to the twenty minutes twice a day and build up to the 40 minutes once again.

If you find yourself at a crossroad, things are just not going well, and you are not sure of your path, then doing a very long meditation can be most enlightening. No eating during the meditation, small sips of water are allowed. It is best if you can be out in nature. Then either sit or stand for a minimum of two hours. Nothing really happens the first two hours – for some people it takes more than two hours. Continue to meditate. After a while your sense of space and time will go away, the trees and rocks will begin to talk to you. Even the shadows will move and talk. All other sounds will go away. Animals may show up and talk with you. Spirits will show up and talk with you. In the end the path you need to follow will be very clear.

People who use drugs are at risk for damaging their chakras. If you suspect this may have happened to you then meditation will help to straighten out your energy field. It may also be helpful to go to an experienced healer and have some subtle energy healing work done as well. Drinking alcohol and smoking has a negative effect on people's ability to meditate as well. If you can stop drinking and / or smoking altogether that is best. If you cannot stop drinking and / or smoking, then meditate first and drink later.

Remember that if you have thoughts during meditation it simply means that you are human - even the greatest yogis have thoughts. As you become aware of the thought learn to just simply note the thought and go back to your anchor. Beating yourself because you have thoughts during meditation is not productive and will only create barriers to future meditation.

Remember there is no good or bad meditation - only meditations that you do or do not do. Keep meditating daily, no matter what happened during the previous meditation. If you miss a day, week, month, year, or years simply start meditating once more. It is important to develop a meditation practice. What this means for you will vary depending on your reason for meditating and the amount of time you are willing to devote to the practice. The important aspect of a meditation practice is that it be regular. If you only meditate once a week then always meditate once a week, on the same day, at the same time. If you meditate daily, then again do so at the same time every day. Eventually it will be like an exercise program in that you will really notice when you missed your regular practice session.

When you have a meditation where you go very deep or have great insights, simply appreciate it and let go of attachments, as not all meditations will be like that. If you become attached to the deep meditation and expect it every time you run the risk of being disappointed in the meditation process. "Let go and let God". Just meditate without expectations or attachments.

It is normal for people to go through different stages of meditation. Sometimes there are long periods that are challenging. It usually means you are about to go through a transition so hang in there. Again, let go of expectations. A good meditation is the meditation that you do.

Look for and document any miracles that occur in your life. Meditation will open up your awareness of miracles and you will find yourself becoming a part of the miracles. A daily diary or journal is a great way to capture these events. Add them to your gratitude practice.

Learning to bring your soul into your body helps you to know you are part of a larger whole. When you do not bring our soul into our body you feel detached. This is the root source of loneliness and sadness. Knowing your soul purpose and path for this life helps you to feel attached. Why not have your soul enter your body at any time? - You can get spaced out. Once you are able to stay grounded while meditating, then you can begin to bring the soul into your body at any time during the day and practice keeping it there. The soul is not the same as your aura or energy field. This is an energy of its own, your spiritual soul, versus your body soul. Hold your soul as high in your body as possible. Above the head is best. Sometimes you have to send it down to your first chakra then bring it up one chakra at a time until it is at your crown chakra. Hold it there all day, even while talking. This is a challenging and very advanced practice. It requires that you stay in a meditative state all day and that everything you do and say is from your spiritual center and comes from your heart. When I first started doing this it would wear me out. It is a lot of work, however, when you are ready this is an awesome way to always be connected to your higher self and speak only from your heart.

Energy grids

Energy grids help the energy in a room or space to run at higher vibrations and with more volume. To set up a grid, first clear the space. You can use sage, incense, baking powder, a candle, and energy system, or just by intention. Then set the Dharma boundaries by paying homage to the four directions. It is important to do the above whenever spiritual work will be done. I also like to place a lotus under the floor as well, again do this by your intention.

Stages of Meditation:

Over the span of one's life there can be many stages of meditation. Typically, the first phase is to develop a habit – this takes from two months to two years for most people. The next phase is to let go of attachments. This will be the most challenging for most people as they are not even aware of the attachment. You may experience seeing lights, images, or have unusual experiences, let them go and do not become attached to them. Everyone will have these experiences so expect them once in a while. The idea is to not get caught up in the experience but to remain detached. This will take anywhere from two months to ten years to a lifetime. With detachment comes enlightenment, past life memories, future life memories, tremendous knowledge, inner peace, and much more.

In Closing

All things are possible for all people. Meditation is the tool that opens all doors of possibility, removing all obstacles, healing all issues, all the while bringing profound inner peace. Meditation is the cornerstone of all spiritual practices - the basis through which understanding and inner knowing is manifested. Only you can heal yourself. Only you can do the work to advance spiritually. A guru or teacher can only show you a way, you are the only one who can help yourself. Everything external is just a teacher or guide and cannot give you "the answer" for your life. Only you can create your answer for yourself and meditation is the best vehicle for most people to use to accomplish this worthy goal.

May your path be filled with light,
May your heart be filled with love,
May your mind be filled with peace,
May your life be filled with bliss.
May you always walk with God.
-Dancing Bear

Appendix A - Glossary

Anchor: the focus of a meditation

Empowerment: also known as attunement, download, or Shakti – allows the recipient to bring in a specific energy

Bliss: that divine state that transcends all else when the observed and observer are one

Posture: how one sits / stands / moves - different postures produce different results

Religion: A practice of worship of a being or God(s) in the form of various rituals, prayers and related activities. *"the feelings, acts, and experiences of individual men in their solitude, so far as they apprehend themselves to stand in relation to whatever they may consider the divine"* by William James *"what the individual does with his own solitariness"* by Alfred North Whitehead, Harvard Professor

Both of the above quotes are from *On Searching the Scriptures—Your Own or Someone Else's* by Jaroslav Pelikan

Spiritual: the highest level of self above the physical, emotional, and mental planes. It involves the understanding of soul or higher self, the part of us that is dreaming, our 3-D life experience.

Appendix B - Bibliography

* Means highly recommend

Web links:

Note: that the web is ever changing. It cannot be promised that these links still exist, only that they existed at one time. Many are no longer available but still listed in the event they have changed and are recognized by the reader.

Aina.org www.aina.org/books/eog/eog.pdf - *The Epic of Gilgamesh*

Angel Therapy www.angeltherapy.com – Dr. Doreen Virtue's web site on angels

* Dancing Bear Way www.dancingbearway.com – notes on meditation, shamanism, esoteric energy, healing, and other spiritual practices (Note: this site is also known as www.dancing-bear.com, when the "-" is not used it takes you to a porn site so another name was created)

Dzogchen.org www.Dzogchen.org – definition and information on the Dzogchen practice

Foundation for Shamanic Studies www.shamanism.org – information on shamanism and their class schedule

* Healing Mantras https://duckduckgo.com/l/?kh=-1&uddg=https%3A%2F%2Fpatricialohan.com%2Fwp-content%2Fuploads%2F2014%2F04%2FHealing-Mantras.pdf – Healing Mantras by Thomas Ashley-Farrand

Isis http://isis.infinet.com/rinpoche/sutra.htm – Buddhist Sutras and mantras

Meditative Mind www.youtube.com/watch?v=eBopONbgNpQ – Green Tara Mantra

Mahakatha – Meditation Mantras www.youtube.com/watch?v=wlZqghmN24U – Tayata Om Mantra Dzogchen Chant

Maharishi University of Management www.miu.edu/ - TM

Pro Liberty www.proliberty.com/yoga/mantras.html – holy mantras

Samantabhadra & Samantabhadri https://soonyata.home.xs4all.nl/sorubasamadhi.htm - information on Rainbow body

Sanskrit Mantras www.sanskritmantra.com/simple.htm – mantras

Shambhala Resources http://apk.net/~dizzy/resources.html - books and supplies

TM Organization www.tm.org/research-on-meditation - Research on meditation

Wikipedia https://en.wikipedia.org/wiki/Dzogchen - Wikipedia definition of Dzogchen

World Breath Meditation http://world.std.com/~metta/ftp/modern/breathmed.html – breath meditation

Yoga, Tantra and Meditation in Daily Life http://scand-yoga.org/uk_book.htm

Meditation:

Ashley-Farrand, Thomas, *Healing Mantras* Sounds True, Boulder, CO, 1999

Cooper, Rabbi David A., *The Mystical Kabbalah*, Sounds True, Colorado, 1994 – 5 audio cassettes

* Goleman, Daniel, *The Meditative Mind*, G.P Putnam's Sons, New York, 1988 - Excellent overview, including, states of mind, research, and various paths

Goleman, Daniel, *The Varieties of the Meditative Experience*, Irvington Publishers, New York, 1978

Goleman, Daniel, *The Vibrations of the Meditative Experience*, Irvington Publishers, Inc, New York, 1977

Excellent overview of the different religious and cultural meditative practices (read only if you dare)

* Kabat-Zinn, Jon, *Wherever You Go There You Are - Mindfulness Meditation in Everyday Life*, Hyperion, New York, 1994 - Breathe meditation and dealing with stress

Feuerstein, G. *The Deeper Dimension of Yoga.* Shambala Publications, Boston, MA. 2003

Kunsang, Erik Pema, Schmidt, Marcia Binder, *Quintessential Dzogchen, Confusion Dawns as Wisdom*, Rangjung Yeshe Publications, Hong Kong, 2006

Lamrimpa, Gen, *Calming the Mind*, Snow Lion Publications, New York, 1934 - (Tibetan Buddhist)

* Novak, John, *How to Meditate*, Crystal & Clarity Publishers, California, 1989

Includes posture, visualization, chanting, movement, breathing, and the affect on the chakras

Paulson Genevieve Lewis, *Meditation and Human Growth*, Llewellyn Publications, Minnesota, 1994 - Easy to understand

Richards, Steve, *Levitation*, Aquarian/Thorsons, London, 1990 - Lots of info on TM

Rinpoche, Tulku Urgyen, *Rainbow Painting*, Rangjung Yeshe Publications, Hong Kong, 1995 – "A Collection of Miscellaneous Aspects of Development and Completion"

Esoteric Healing:

Bailey, Alice, *Esoteric Healing - Volume IV A Treatise on the Seven Rays*, Lucas Press, London, 1993

Brennan, Barbara Ann, *Hands of Light - A Guide to Healing Through the Human Energy_Field*, Bantom Books, Rochester, New York, 1988

Brennan, Barbara Ann, *Light Emerging - The Journey of Personal Healing*, Bantom Books, Rochester, New York, 1993

* Chopra, Deepak, MD., *Quantum Healing - Exploring the Frontiers of Mind/Body Medicine,* Bantom Books, Rochester, New York, 1990

Chopra, Deepak, MD., *Perfect Health - the Complete Mind/Body Guide*, Harmony Books, New York, 1992

Horan, Paula, *Empowerment Through Reiki* - the path to personal and global transformation, Lotus Light, Wisconsin, 1992

Rand, William L., *Reiki - the Healing Touch - First and Second degree Manual*, Vision Publications, Missouri, 1991

Rapgay, Dr. Lpsang, *The Tibetan Book of Healing,* Passage Press, Utah, 1996 - The elements and using them with healing

Walker, Dael, *The Crystal Healing Book - How to Use Crystals for Healing and Personal Growth,* Crystal Company, California, 1988

* Weil, Andrew, MD., *Spontaneous Healing - How to Discover and Enhance Your Body's Natural Ability to Maintain and Heal Itself,* Alfred A. Knopf, New York, 1995

The Big Picture:

Bailey, Alice, *Initiation, Human and Solar,* Lucas Press, London, 1992

* Foundation for Inner Peace, *A Course in Miracles,* Foundation for Inner Peace, California, 1992

Golas, Thaddeus, *The Lazy Man's Guide to Enlightenment,* Bantom, New York, 1972

Miller, Barbara Stoler, *The Bhagavad-Gita - Krishna's Counsel in Time of War,* Bantom Books, New York, 1986

Pelikan, Jaroslav, *On Searching the Scriptures—Your Own or Someone Else's,* Quality Paperback Book Club, New York, 1992, Understanding the sacred writings

Radhakrishnan, S., *The Principal Upanishads,* Humanities Press, New Jersey, 1993

* Two Disciples, *Rainbow Bridge* Volume II, Rainbow Bridge Productions, California 1982

Shamanism and Huna:

Castaneda, Carlos, *The Teachings of Don Juan - Yaqui Way of Knowledge,* The University of California Press, California, 1994

Dow, JaneAnn, *Crystal Journey - Travel Guide for the New Shaman,* Journey Books, New Mexico, 1992

Foster, Steven, *Vision Quest - Personal Transformation in the Wilderness,* Fireside, New York, 1992

* Harner, Michael, *The Way of the Shaman,* Harper, San Francisco, 1990

Ingerman, Sandra, *Soul Retrieval - Mending the Fragmented Self*, Harper, San Francisco, 1991

Ingerman, Sandra, *Welcome Home - Life After Healing, Following Your Soul's Journey Home*, Harper, San Francisco, 1993

King, Serge Kahili, *Kahuna Healing*, Theosophical Publishing, Illinois, 1992

* Millman, Dan, *Sacred Journey of the Peaceful Warrior*, HJ Kramer, California, 1991

Moondance, Wolf, *Rainbow Medicine - A Visionary Guide to Native American Shamanism*, Sterling Publishing, New York, 1994

Stevens, Jose, Ph.D. & Lena S., *Secrets of Shamanism - Tapping the Spirit Power in You*, Avon Books, New York, 1988

Walsh, Roger, Ph.D., *The Spirit of Shamanism*, Jeremy P. Tarcher, Los Angeles, 1990

Miscellaneous:

Bailey, Alice, *The Rays and The Initiations*, Lucas Press, London, 1960

Beyerl, Paul V., *A Wican Bardo*, Prisim Unity, 1989 - Initiation and Self-Transformation

* Bucke, Richard Maurice MD., *Cosmic Consciousness - A Study in the Evolution of the Human Mind* - The Classic Investigation of the Development of Man's Mystic Relation to the Infinite, Arkana, New York, 1989 (first published in 1893)

Campbell, Dan, *Edgar Cayce on the Power of Color, Stones, and Crystals*, Warner Books, New York, 1989

Campbell, Joseph, *The Portable JUNG*, Penguin Books, New York, 1971

* Chopra, Deepak, MD., *Ageless Body Timeless Mind - the Quantum Alternative to Growing Old*, Harmony Books, New York, 1993

Chopra, Deepak, MD., *Perfect Weight*, Random House, New York, 1994

Evans-Wentz, W.Y., *The Tibetan Book of the Dead*, Oxford University Press, London, 1960

Freidlander, Joel, Body Types, *The Enneagram of Essence Types,* Inner Journey Books, San Rafael, 1986

Gabriel, Michael, M.A., <u>*Voices from the Womb*</u>, Aslan Publishing, California, 1992

Gardner, Joy, *Color and Crystals - a Journey Through the Chakras*, The Crossing Press, California, 1988

* Jampolsky, Gerald, MD., *Love is Letting Go of Fear*, Celestial Arts, California, 1979

Jampolsky, Gerald, MD., *Love is the Answer - Creating Positive Relationships*, Bantom Books, New York, 1990

*Jeffers, Susan, Ph.D., *Feel the Fear and Do It Anyway* - Dynamic techniques for turning fear, indecision, and anger into Poser, Action, and Love, Fawcett Columbine, New York, 1987

Kingsland, Venika Mehra, *The Simple Guide to Hinduism*, Global Books Limited, England, 1997

McNichol, Andrea, *Handwriting Analysis, Putting It to Work for You*, Contemporary Books, Chicago, 1991

Miller, Barbara Stoler (Translation), *The Bhagavad-Gita*, Bantam Books, New York, 1986

Olyanova, Nadia, *The Psychology of Handwriting - the Secrets of Handwriting Analysis*, Wilshire Book Co., California, 1960

Robertson, Robin, *After the End of Time - Revelation and the Growth of Consciousness*, Inner Vision, Virginia, 1990

Rodgers, Vimala, *Change Your Handwriting, Change Your Life*, Celestial Arts, California, 1993

Roman, Klara G., *Handwriting - A Key to Personality*, Pantheon Books, New York, 1952

Sanders, Pete, *You Are Psychic* - An MIT-trained scientist's proven program for expanding your psychic powers, Fawcett Powers, New York, 1989

Index

S

T

V

Y

Appendix C - About the Author

Dancing Bear, Ph.D., L.Ac., is a metaphysician, licensed acupuncturist, author, lecturer, and spiritual practitioner. She is the founder of the Dancing Bear Healing Center and the author of the www.dancingbearway.com web site. Dancing Bear also has created recordings of workshops and tapes with guided imagery.

Dancing Bear is a Reiki Master who is initiated in to the Usui (Japanese), and Tibetan Reiki systems. She was gifted *Green Goddess Reiki* from Green Tara, *Ankh of Isis* from Isis, and *Staff of Osiris* from Osiris, energy systems. She has also been initiated into many other esoteric healing energy and meditation systems from various mystery schools she has attended.

Dancing Bear is a graduate of the three-year shaman training program offered by the Foundation of Shamanic Studies and has studied the shamanic practices of many cultures including, Huna, Celtic, Tuvan, and Native American (Cherokee).

Dancing Bear is certified as a Handwriting Consultant. Handwriting analysis is used as an adjunct therapy to her hypnotherapy and healing practice.

Dancing Bear is a certified Colorpuncture practitioner who uses colored light to help facilitate the bodies energy to heal oneself. She also uses sound healing with tuning forks, recordings, as well as mantras to facilitate the healing process.

NOTES

NOTES

Printed in the United States
By Bookmasters